SHAME

Carrie Anne

A Green Flame Omnimedia Slim

Based entirely on truth.

Anne, Carrie — 1st Green Flame Omnimedia edition

SHAME: Something to Heal or Disallow?/Carrie Anne

Summary: A descent into poverty is something the author felt as ashamed of as the few times she slept with people she was not attracted to...but are the causes of these kinds of shame the same?

Trade paperback Slim
ISBN-13: 978-1540833150; ISBN-10: 1540833151

1. Poverty 2. Shame 3. Interpersonal Relationships 4. Economics
5. Depression/Recession 6. Oppression 7. Hungarian Jews
8. Food Pantries 9. Charity 10. Auschwitz 11. Personal Growth 12. Integrity
13. Spiritual Growth 14. Societal Change

Green Flame Omnimedia
Postal Suite 783
Volcano Hawaii 9678

I stood in line for my neighborhood's food pantry unsure how much longer I would have to be doing this...how much longer I would be *able* to...do this.

It wasn't that things weren't still financially rocky for me, so I could still certainly use the monthly infusion of free food...

And clearly I wasn't alone...wasn't the only person not making it, as evidenced by the fact that I was waiting on a long line.

But as a person who had once been successful, in this area and elsewhere in the world, I found this entire experience of accepting charity excruciating.

Especially when a woman I knew peripherally (someone I *knew!*) from local activist circles approached the line, deep in conversation on her iPhone.

I felt the flush of shame

rise.

Which is not just a blushing cheek...not just a gentle embarrassment that can be quite fetching and even endearing in certain circumstances.

The flush of shame is an all over toxic body heat that uncomfortably warms while simultaneously chilling your body from the roots of your hair down through your innards and limbs all the way to the fat, sizzling tips of your toes.

And feeling it here,

waiting on a food pantry line, was not dissimilar from the awful kinds of heat I'd experienced on the few occasions I'd become lovers with someone I hadn't actually wanted to be naked with...(someone I then would rather have died than been seen with in public, afterwards).

When the poison of shame engulfs me, I am always glad I have brown skin so it is still somewhat invisible even in public...unless those around me are good at reading sinking auras or body language.

Though I had also benefited, briefly, from the charitable supplies of other food pantries in my area, most of them required trackable information: name, age, ID, etc.

Which I was unwilling to give. So I lied. And stopped going there.

It is one thing to accept free food when you're starving...and quite another to be on record forevermore for doing so.

So I had not applied for food stamps or any other kind

of official aid, though my circumstances surely would have qualified...and I only went to places willing to provide help without requiring anyone's life story.

You'd be amazed how few and far between this kind of no-strings help actually is.

Did bread lines during the Great Depression or the Dust Bowl era require people to prove they needed help?

If so, why?

It's hard enough to admit you need help in the first place...never mind having to be scrutinized and labeled in order to receive it.

Therefore, I was ecstatic when I saw in the paper a Convoy of Hope event that was coming through our local sports stadium one weekend in order to provide not only free food but also clothing and potential job services and free entertainment to our economically depressed area...without requiring IDs.

Though the job booth didn't have any leads I could realistically apply for (being someone who no longer had access to a working car or means to purchase a new one, in an area with scant public transportation), I *was* able to haul home 40 lbs of Science Diet cat food in rain-proof black plastic trash bags bungie-corded to a wagon for the long bus ride (followed by a 40 minute hike) back home.

The cats were very happy and well fed that day.

The Convoy of Hope event also had free 15-minute chair massages, and having my tense shoulders and neck touched brought tears to my eyes.

"Student massages are only $35 for an hour at our

Academy," the masseuse told me as I stood up, shaky and grateful.

And I nodded.

Back in the days when I was more reliably earning income and had money to spare, I used to frequent our local massage school's students for regular full-body nurturing.

But that was back when $35 did not mean the difference in being able to keep the electricity on...or not.

So, waiting for this

month's local food pantry's helping of canned beef stew, a handful of bananas and energy bars, a crushed box of off-brand cereal, concentrated cranberry juice, and a ziplock bag of rice, I stared past the line at a playground of slides and colorful tunnels where a variety of children — some of whose parents were probably also waiting on line — shrieked and shouted, shame-free.

Growing up, my single parent household didn't have much in the way of money, but we did always have some kind of supermarket and health food store purchased foods in the refrigerator and cupboards to eat, every single day.

Until I became an adult myself — responsible for things like income always meeting, and hopefully surpassing, one's expenses, — I don't think I ever realized how difficult this feat could be.

I don't recall waiting with my mother on any kind of charity lines throughout my formative years, though my father often missed or was late sending child support.

Perhaps she stood on lines I never knew about...since being a parochial school Kindergarten teacher did entail always receiving a salary below poverty level...even back in the days when the dollar held more value than it does today.

(To wit: I earned around the same annual almost $20K salary upon landing my first-ever, corporate, post-college-graduation job as my Mom earned upon gold-star retiring after 25 years of parochial school service.)

One previous month

during my fall from Grace onto food pantry lines, upon leaving with two bulging bags of free food, I'd bumped, literally, into a spiritual teacher I'd studied with years ago...

And though this was quite the surprise for both of us, we had been able to hug and I had managed to bluster my way through a sunshine-y offer to sit together and catch up over the hot meal about to be served by the same food pantry folk, after putting my bags of supplies away in the car a neighbor was now so very generously letting me borrow once a month, since my own had stopped working.

(Side note: my own car was subsequently stolen from right outside my home, making pitiful attempts to try and save up enough of the barely-coming-in-at-all money to eventually have it fixed, obsolete.)

But my spiritual teacher shook her head and said she wasn't staying for the sit down hot meal...and I did my best not to notice that, as a white woman, her cheeks had begun flushing a sorrowful crimson.

Besides her, up until this

day, months later, I hadn't seen anyone else I knew or recognized on the food pantry line...and I had felt somewhat resignedly-but-securely invisible...surrounded by my new community of neighborhood down-&-outs.

So suddenly spotting someone else I knew from a previous, less-destitute era of my life, someone who was now standing somewhere behind me on line and had likely spotted me too, caused me to once again heat up from head to toe with an all over desire to be anywhere but where I was.

And, with the line moving as glacially slow as it was, this return of toxic heat forced me to remember some of what I'd been painstakingly learning about metaphysical truths, and how to turn seemingly insurmountable situations around.

I reached for gratitude.

I was thankful that there *was* a no-ID-necessary food pantry in my neck of the woods, and that I had access to a vehicle for the day in order to get to it (and do things like laundry too!).

I was grateful that I had recently seen this other woman at an artsy event where chatting over the latest movies had been able to happen, no shame involved.

In fact, it was this very woman who had steered me towards making sure I saw Meryl Streep in the unusual *Florence Foster Jenkins* film that explored a human being's right to put forth music they loved...even if they sang badly.

A movie I'd enjoyed several times on DVD by then

with friends.

So when I departed the food pantry supply room, bulging bags in tow, and came face to face on my way out with this acquaintance who was now at the entryway awaiting her turn (couldn't have timed this better if we'd tried, of course), I was able to sincerely thank her for the film recommendation...rather than the two of us bobbing awkwardly, bodies flaming, around the fact that we — who had once had the world seemingly by the tail, being well-paid for doing interesting

things in this community —
were now both in the unlucky
position of having to wait on a
line for handouts.

I put the free food I was
grateful for into my
neighbor's car, and headed
back inside for the warm
meal.

A meal I hadn't had to
shop for, purchase, or cook,
and wouldn't have to clean up
after.

I continued to hold my
head intentionally high in
gratitude as I accepted
spoonfuls of mashed potatoes
and kale and salad and bread.

And when the woman chose to come sit at my table, we carried on with a lively *Florence Foster Jenkins* dialog, drawing in the gentlemen, one white, one black, seated nearby.

And then a friend I had met at these free hot meals months ago bounded up to our table with a little present wrapped in a cheery greeting card for me, and I felt a different kind of warmth.

Not dissimilar from my younger days when I had laughed with new college friends around animated cafeteria tables, sharing the day's trials and tribulations, and feeling surprisingly bubbly and popular for a bookworm...excited for the adventures ahead.

So what if the world was going to hell in a hand-basket, and I didn't have a car or enough money or any idea how to really get my life back on its feet?

I *did* still have a rustic roof over my head, 4 great cats, some food for all of our bellies, and a soft, warm glow in my body that, at the moment at least, was not from being ashamed.

Days later, a piece of tooth cracked off in my mouth, and I wasn't even biting into anything hard.

But there it was, spit into my palm amidst soggy chunks of garlic bread.

I'd been saving these bits of tooth and fillings in my jewelry box over the past several years, I don't know what for.

It's not like I would be going to a dentist any time soon to show evidence of what needs to be refilled or capped over.

Right now I can't even afford toothpaste, so I finished eating and then brushed my teeth in a dilution of hydrogen peroxide and water, feeling the demon Shame try to rear up and catch hold.

So what, I/it thought, *now I'll even start looking like a poverty-stricken, semi-toothless, old hag as I stand on the bread lines?! Shit!!!*

But I spit and rinsed and then checked my smile over the sink in the bathroom mirror. So far the teeth that

have been going, including
this one, have been way in the
back of my mouth, so my
smile still looks white,
youthful, whole.

It's not like my mouth
hasn't had issues before in my
entire life; a few of the teeth
that comprise my bright white
smile are actually composite-
over-gold caps from a less
Western, more holistic dentist
I used to travel overnight to
for pain-free, very costly
appointments.

But I'd made a
commitment to myself years
ago — even before financial

circumstances necessitated —
to begin practicing a more
holistic sense of health care
overall, rather than
continuing to try and
medicate one type of
seemingly dire illness or
another.

And, for the most part,
this has worked out well for
me and I no longer even catch
colds.

Which has been a good
thing...for many reasons...not
the least of which is: I feel
blessed by a glow in my
cheeks from whatever the
opposite of shame is
whenever I am able to hold

my head high from demonstrating evidence that I am taking good care of myself...my whole self...naturally.

Because that's what Shame is all about, isn't it?

Seemingly a need for secrecy.

A compulsion to keep broken parts of one's self hidden.

As if needing free food or an inability to afford dental care is an indication of some fatal failing in my own self and life...rather than a byproduct of a social structure that regularly leads to economic and civil downturns that, like clockwork, cause people to stand on bread lines, unable to afford many things that they need.

But with one out of every three individuals murdered at Auschwitz being a Hungarian Jew, people like Zoltan Dückstein must have felt grateful to find himself, for a time, teaching gymnasium (European high school) Phys

Ed...even if that was a far cry from the brilliant successes of previously having led a Hungarian Olympic team to victory in boxing, wrestling, fencing, and water polo back in 1932.

This new era of his life as an ordinary Phys Ed instructor might have seemed like a tremendous fall from Grace...back before social and civil and economic laws changed where he lived, leading to things like Auschwitz... and most likely making him *very* grateful in that moment to have any kind of job and life at all.

People can always do something about choosing *not* to personally sleep with anyone they aren't actually attracted to, thus avoiding a need to heal from that kind of personal Shame...but whether or not a person *can* feasibly earn enough income to meet their and their family's needs in a corrupt, violent, economically devastated and/or oppressive era (such as those that regularly seem to take hold everywhere on Planet Earth) is maybe not something we are supposed to *individually* burn with shame

about?

Maybe those kinds of societal shames are what have really fallen from Grace...and are something everyone should resist...and — like with the pervasive shames involved in our current corporate-crook culture, for example — maybe those kinds of shames are something we should all do our darndest not to personally take in, but rather help change...whether we are the ones who find ourselves standing on bread lines...or not.

ABOUT THE AUTHOR

More of Carrie Anne's life adventures are featured in the *Wombeing Wisdom Illustrated Guide to Evolution*, available in color or black/white print as well as e-editions: https://www.amazon.com/Wombeing-Wisdom-Metaphysical-Guidance-Evolution-ebook/dp/B018NGEK9O

www.ingramcontent.com/pod-product-compliance
Lightning Source LLC
Chambersburg PA
CBHW021449170526
45164CB00001B/450